KEYS for MARRIAGE

DR. MYLES MUNROE

KEYS for MARRIAGE

WHITAKER
HOUSE

KEYS FOR MARRIAGE

(revised and updated edition of *Marriage 101,* originally published by Pneuma Life Publishing)

ISBN-13: 978-1-60374-030-2
ISBN-10: 1-60374-030-9
Printed in the United States of America
© 1999, 2008 by Dr. Myles Munroe

Whitaker House
1030 Hunt Valley Circle
New Kensington, PA 15068
www.whitakerhouse.com

Library of Congress Cataloging-in-Publication Data (pending)

1 2 3 4 5 6 7 8 9 10 11 12 **ᴜ** 16 15 14 13 12 11 10 09 08

INTRODUCTION

*M*ales and females have different—but perfectly complementary—designs. The secret to a successful marriage is to recognize, support, and benefit from these harmonious purposes. It is to help one's spouse, through unconditional love, to become all God created him or her to be.

Where purpose is not known, abuse is inevitable. No matter how serious you are about your marriage, if you don't know the reason why it exists, you will abuse it in some way. *Keys for Marriage* introduces you to God's plan for husbands and wives and provides biblical principles you can immediately put into practice in your own marriage. As you grow to be the couple God designed you to be, you will discover firsthand the truth of the Scripture, *"They shall become one flesh"* (Genesis 2:24).

—*Dr. Myles Munroe*

*E*verything in life has a purpose.
Understanding the inherent, God-given
purpose for the male and female will
enlighten your understanding
of your spouse.

*I*f you bought a camera without proper training on how to use it—and you completely disregarded the manual—you'd be foolish to get angry when you couldn't operate it. It is just as foolish to try to operate a marriage without reading its proper manual, the Bible.

KEYS for MARRIAGE

Therefore shall a man leave his father and his mother, and shall cleave unto his wife: and they shall be one flesh" (Genesis 2:24 KJV). Men, you are to leave your mother and father and cleave to the woman you marry. The result? You and your wife become one flesh.

Marriage is when two separate, unique, and whole persons (one male, one female) make a covenant to exchange vows, committing themselves to remain together until death.

$\mathcal{W}$hen you continually place your parents'
opinions and views before your spouse's, you
are planting seeds of destruction, and you
will eat the fruit of divorce.

The boundary that God has established for the one-flesh experience is the husband and wife relationship. Marriage enables us to enjoy sex to the fullest. Sex is a physical sign of a spiritual act—the giving of oneself completely to another and for another.

God did not initiate the human race by putting a parent and child in the garden of Eden. He put Adam and Eve there—husband and wife. That shows that the primary human relationship, the family, is husband and wife, and they are the key to every other relationship.

$\mathcal{U}$nderstanding and living in God's original purpose for men and women is crucial for right relationships between husbands and wives. If we fight against God's purpose, we will be unfulfilled and frustrated. He made us the way we are for His purposes and our benefit.

God created men and women equal, and He created them different. "Different" doesn't mean one is inferior or superior to the other; it simply means different. The differences between men and women are necessary because of their God-given purposes.

$\mathcal{M}$ales and females are not different because of society, environment, or family upbringing; they are different by design. Husbands, this means your wife is the way she is because of why she is. Likewise, wives, your husband is the way he is because of why he is.

Keys for Marriage

*B*ecause God is love, His plans embody
what is best for us. His purpose requires
two sexes working together in cooperation
to accomplish a mutual vision. Accordingly,
males and females have complementary
designs that enable them to fulfill
God's purpose together.

$\mathcal{T}$he biblical functions of an effective husband are to…

- Worship
- Work
- Cultivate
- Protect
- Teach

Any male not carrying out these functions is malfunctioning.

*H*usbands, in order to be the provider God created you to be, you must have two things—a vision and the means for provision.

Where there is no vision, the people perish: but he that keepeth the law, happy is he" (Proverbs 29:18 KJV). Having a family vision is so important that if you don't have it, there will be no discipline. It keeps you alive, focused, and on course.

A husband's purpose is to lead, teach, and stay in the presence of the Lord so that he can know where his family is going and where they should be going.

A husband without a clear purpose and vision for his life makes for a frustrated wife. Your wife is a helpmate, but if you're not doing anything, how can you expect your wife to help with it?

When you have two totally opposite and separate visions within one home, you have division, which leads to divorce. Jesus said, *"Every kingdom divided against itself is brought to desolation, and every city or house divided against itself will not stand"* (Matthew 12:25).

*M*en, you will never start off with the woman you want; that's why you are cultivators. Your job is to cultivate your wife so she can be all God created her to be. You need to nurture all the potential she has.

KEYS for MARRIAGE

*H*ow do you envision your wife and
what do you think she can be? Whatever you
envision for her is what you will cultivate.

Too many husbands grumble about the kind of wife they wish they had. You want her to look nice? Buy clothes for her! You want her to have a nice hairstyle? Pay for her to go to the beauty salon! You want her in shape? Go with her to the gym!

A husband should give up his egocentric desires in order to serve his wife and family. A real man takes care of others before himself.

"The woman is the glory of the man" (1 Corinthians 11:7 KJV). The glory of something is its true nature or best expression of itself. The sun is in its glory when it shines at noon, and husbands are in their glory when their wives are radiant.

*H*usbands have a great responsibility to reflect the image of God so that this can be reflected to their wives and their wives can reflect God's image in turn.

$\mathcal{M}$ en, as cultivators, you are supposed to make everything you touch better than it was when you first encountered it. Find new ways to help make your wife better.

*M*en, you were built to handle tough things. No matter how rough it gets, know that you've got the right stuff to handle it and work out each problem. God designed you to come through every storm.

*H*usbands, when the time comes to lead your family through challenging situations, step up and say, "I am an overcomer! Nothing can overcome me." *"I have written to you, young men, because you are strong, and the word of God abides in you, and you have overcome the wicked one"* (1 John 2:14).

*Y*our wife should always know that no matter what happens, you're not going to fold up or be afraid of difficulty because you've got what it takes to make it through.

Someone may say, "Brother, is your woman at home giving you grief? Let's go get a drink." No, you go home. Men of purpose understand that anything that numbs their minds and slows down their logical thinking processes is an enemy to themselves and their families.

*A*ny man who comes home, grabs his wife by the collar, and shouts, "Woman, you haven't cooked my food yet?" should expect his next meal to be poison.

*M*en, if you're beating up your wife and children, STOP IT! God didn't give you strength to abuse your family members. He gave you that strength to protect them. They should feel secure every time you show up, not afraid.

There are many guys who can shoot
a three-pointer but can't bring up their
children or sustain a family. They haven't
learned how to take that same drive
and channel it properly through
the Word of God.

For God so loved the world that He gave His only begotten Son..." (John 3:16).
God exposed the true nature of love. Because He loved, He gave. You cannot love without giving.

$\mathscr{M}$ales and females should respect and love one another. Jesus reinforced this principle when He said one of the greatest commandments is *"Love your neighbor as yourself"* (Matthew 19:19). If we really understood this truth, there would be more patience, understanding, and forgiveness among men and women.

$\mathcal{O}$ur family relationships can be restored in Jesus Christ. God wants to bring His life-changing power to broken marriages, damaged families, and individuals who need reconciliation with God and a restoration of His purposes for them.

$\mathcal{L}$ove is stronger than pride.

Be brave enough to break down the walls

that barricade your spouse from your heart.

A dog is not a man's best friend! A dog cannot tell you your faults or point out your weaknesses. How cowardly it is to allow your pet to become the object of your affections rather than your spouse.

When God made woman, He drew her out of man so the man would have someone to love who was of the same nature. It was love that brought about the woman's existence.

et each one of you in particular so love his own wife as himself, and let the wife see that she respects her husband" (Ephesians 5:33). Nowhere does the Bible tell the wife to love the husband, but to honor and respect him. Yet the husband is told to love the wife. Why? The Lord knows our greatest needs.

No husband should ever be intimidated or insecure when his wife makes more money than he does. When security marries insecurity, problems occur because that man identifies his position with possessions rather than the potential God placed in him.

A man whose wife makes more money than he does but who is doing his utmost to work a job and help fulfill his wife's spiritual, financial, emotional, and intellectual needs is being a good provider.

Husbands are always to be accountable and responsible. Real men don't play the blame game—always pointing a finger at everyone but themselves.

If you bring your gift to the altar, and there remember that your brother [or your spouse] *has something against you, leave your gift there before the altar, and go your way. First be reconciled to your brother* [spouse], *and then come and offer your gift"* (Matthew 5:23–24).

When something is wrong in your
marriage, it's up to you to make it right.
Don't wait for the other person
to make the first move.

*M*en, as far as God is concerned, you are ready for marriage when you are able to teach your family His Word. If you don't know the Word, you should make it a priority to study and gain knowledge of the Bible. You can't teach what you don't know.

Many Christians love to hide behind God so they don't have to deal with the responsibility of a face-to-face human relationship. Jesus said He is the Way, the Truth, and the Life, but He never said He's your excuse to avoid responsibility.

Three God-given purposes of a woman are enhancer, reflector, and life-giver or "incubator."

The angel said to the women, *"He is risen! He is not here….Go, tell His disciples…"* (Mark 16:6–7). Why didn't God give the resurrection message to men first? They forget too much and don't have the ability to incubate. He spoke to incubators who could take that message and never stop talking about it. Hallelujah!

A woman is gifted with many creative abilities that can assist her loved ones, herself, and the world. She is an entire research and development department all in one. She sees possibilities and potential. She develops ideas and programs. She conceives and invents.

*Y*our wife is an inherent incubator—
she multiplies everything she receives.
Give her a smile, and she'll give you her heart.
Give her sperm, and she'll give you a baby.
Give her a house, and she'll give you a home.
Give her frustration, and…?

*H*usbands, pay attention:
If you take a little idea and drop it into your
wife's mind, you'll never get just an idea
back—you'll get a detailed plan!

$\mathcal{W}$ives, your ability to think, incubate, and come up with plans is supposed to help your husband, but what are you using those abilities for? If you're trying to prove to him that you're just as good as he is, then you're not his helper; you're his competitor.

$\mathcal{I}$f your husband doesn't pray, don't browbeat him by asking, "Why don't you ever get up and pray?" Pray *for* him. *"For the unbelieving husband is sanctified by the wife, and the unbelieving wife is sanctified by the husband"* (1 Corinthians 7:14).

When your husband opens up to you, encourage him. Don't knock him down with arguments and negativity, no matter how right you think you are. *A soft answer turns away wrath, but a harsh word stirs up anger* (Proverbs 15:1).

*Y*our spouse needs to hear sweet words from *you*, not the person lingering by the water cooler! *"Pleasant words are like a honeycomb, sweetness to the soul and health to the bones"* (Proverbs 16:24).

For if a man does not know how to rule his own house, how will he take care of the church of God?" (1 Timothy 3:5). Many people are running around doing work for the church while their homes are in shambles. If you want your church to be effective, get your home in order first.

He who does not love his brother whom he has seen, how can he love God whom he has not seen?" (1 John 4:20). How do you think you're going to save the world if you don't work to save your marriage?

Wives, don't ever get so "spiritual" that you stay away from your home every night of the week going to prayer meetings. Though you think you're seeking the Lord's face, you will be giving the devil an opening into your home. *"Do not give the devil a foothold"* (Ephesians 4:27 NIV).

*B*eing a Christian doesn't give you the license to neglect your spouse. Your first mission field should be your husband or wife. Sometimes, the way we can best love God is by finding ways to uplift and help our families.

$\mathscr{S}$ome men have been told negative things about themselves all their lives, and they just need an encouraging word from their wives. A wife can be a powerful force for good in her husband's life.

The Lord God said, 'It is not good that man should be alone; I will make him a helper comparable to him'" (Genesis 2:18). The wife's first purpose is to be a companion to her husband so he won't be alone.

$\mathcal{Y}$our wife is like a flower that adapts to the soil. You are like the soil. If you don't like what she has been manifesting, then check what you've been feeding her—nutrients or poison. *"Do not be deceived, God is not mocked; for whatever a man sows, that he will also reap"* (Galatians 6:7).

God created your wife to function on love, and if you are not giving your love to her, then you are causing her to malfunction.

The woman is the glory of the man" (1 Corinthians 11:7 KJV). Your wife was made to be your glory and expose what you are like. When she's happy, that's to your credit. If she's always depressed, withdrawn, sad, or grouchy, that tells me a lot about you, too. She is simply manifesting your glory.

God designed you to cultivate your wife like a beautiful tree. If your tree is wilted after a few years, then it isn't her fault. If you've been married for five years or more and she still hasn't blossomed, then you have a poor track record, brother.

A female was created to incubate everything she receives to reproduce after its kind. Sow bitterness into her, and that's what you will reap. Sow love into her, and you'll reap fruit you'll want to keep.

*H*usbands, love your wives, *and do not be bitter toward them*" (Colossians 3:19). Over and over, the Bible commands the husband to love the wife. Why? Because he's a giver, she's a receiver, and when he gives love to her, she comes alive.

Though your husband may not be able to provide you with a castle right away, you should take whatever he provides for you and give life to it. Paint it, add color to it, and place flowers in it. God blessed you with the ability to make that house a home.

$\mathscr{I}$f your husband doesn't know what to do or how to do it, you need to help him. Help him by pushing him into his position, not by taking it away from him. Never emasculate your man.

She does him good and not evil all the days of her life" (Proverbs 31:12). Wives, you must always ask before you act, "Will this do him good?" A good wife will help her husband become all he's supposed to be.

A good woman doesn't look down
on a man because he can't read the Bible
as well as she can. Even if he reads slowly
and mispronounces words, she doesn't feel
insistent to correct him, but keeps his dignity
intact. *"She opens her mouth with wisdom, and
on her tongue is the law of kindness"*
(Proverbs 31:26).

Her children rise up and call her blessed; her husband also, and he praises her" (Proverbs 31:28). Husband, you ought to always praise your wife. Speak well of her and esteem her highly; lift her up with your words; brag about her; magnify the little things she does by making them bigger than life.

Husbands, the words you speak to your wife affect her emotionally. Wives, the words you speak to your husband provide him with information.

*Y*our husband is not looking for emotions. When you want to talk to him, you have to tell him what you think first, before you express what you feel.

*W*hat your wife is thinking is often different from what she is feeling and saying. You need to be patient and work through her emotions to find out what is truly on her mind.

KEYS for MARRIAGE

Many men have great difficulty verbalizing their emotions, especially when they are hurting, depressed, or sad. A wife needs to create an environment that will enable her husband to be free enough to tell her what he is feeling—not cultivate an environment so negative that he won't ever risk revealing himself.

Women, remember that when your husband is talking, he's not telling you what he's feeling; he's telling you what he's thinking. Therefore, don't draw any conclusions without first discovering what he's feeling behind his thinking.

Conversing attentively with your wife fulfills a need within her. Listen to her and show interest in what she's saying.

*N*ever think that by fulfilling a want, you are satisfying a need. A mink coat may be something your wife wants, but it doesn't meet her need. She needs you to talk to her and tell her she's somebody important, special, unique, and everything you've ever dreamed of.

*M*en, take care of your wives. Caring means that you go out of your way to make sure that she has everything she needs— in her way. Caring means that you leave everything you're doing just to make sure she's okay. Anticipate her need and meet it. That's love.

M ay you ever be captivated by her love" (Proverbs 5:19 NIV). Husband, being captivated by your wife's love is a decision you must make. Allow your wife's love to enthrall you. Wife, delight completely in your husband's love.

The male, by virtue of his purpose, has a teaching capacity. The worst thing to do to a teacher is to make him believe he doesn't know anything. When you start making the teacher feel like he has nothing to offer, you are threatening his very nature.

The best thing you can do for a man is to keep saying, "Tell me more." Even if it seems like foolishness, ask him about it. Encourage him to talk and to share his thoughts by listening to what he is saying.

KEYS for MARRIAGE

*Y*ou are not the way you are because
you are married. You were married
the way that you are.

*A*ny man who goes outside his marriage to find the woman he wants is an infidel and an idiot. He will perish from lacking the knowledge that God created him to cultivate his wife into becoming all she can be and all he'll ever desire.

*N*ever underestimate the value of being supportive of each other's goals, aspirations, and dreams. They provide the wings for your spouse to soar like an eagle and truly accomplish all things.

One of the most ridiculous and dangerous things to tell your husband is, "Why don't you be like So-and-so?" Every man is his own being, and he has his own image of himself. Your job is to be supportive of *him*, not the clone you think he should be.

When you tell your husband that you don't need him, you are doing more than just wounding his feelings; you are killing the very heart of his nature. He was designed to sustain and provide for you. It's the essence of his manhood.

The husband is designed to fulfill his purpose; his purpose determines his nature, and his nature determines his needs. If you want your husband to function effectively, then discover and learn to fulfill his needs.

$\mathscr{D}$on't give your spouse what you need. You both have totally opposite needs and will only frustrate each other by assuming the other should be satisfied with what satisfies you.

*H*usbands and wives must work together to address one another's needs. Jesus' great principle, *"It is more blessed to give than to receive"* (Acts 20:35), is vital. As you give and meet the needs of others, you will be blessed.

Whenever you stand praying, if you have anything against anyone, forgive him, that your Father in heaven may also forgive you your trespasses" (Mark 11:25). Forgive and continually keep on forgiving. Unforgiveness not only can kill your marriage, but its stench can also cause your spiritual relationship with God to rot and die.

*I*t doesn't matter how serious you are about God, how much you speak in tongues, or how much Scripture you have memorized—God's reception of your worship, whether it is in giving, praise, administering the kingdom of God, or operating in ministry gifts, is contingent upon your relationships with other people, especially your spouse.

Call your wife every day and check to make sure everything is okay. Some men check on the sports scores or the Dow Jones average more than they check on their wives. They have the right spirit but the wrong target.

It is shameful when men continually distance themselves from their wives and interpret their help and reaching out as being distrustful or a nuisance. Such men are ignorant of both their wives' purpose and their own needs.

*I*f your wife asks, "Where are you going? What are you doing? Why did you take so long?" she isn't being nosey. She is the way she is because of why she is. What could be so secretive that your helper cannot help you with it?

*I*f your wife can't help you, she'll find something else to help. Ever wonder why the church is filled with so many women? Their husbands don't have a vision for their homes; therefore, the women go to the churches and help the ministers fulfill their visions.

A lot of women are filled with the bitterness their husbands have been pouring into them over the years. Unless their husbands repent and shower them with an abundance of love to wash away such poison, they'll reap what they have sown. *"Husbands, love your wives and do not be bitter toward them"* (Colossians 3:19).

What season is your wife in? When it's summer, the sun is at high noon and hot. When autumn comes, things have cooled a bit. When it's winter, you're out in the cold! But suddenly, spring comes and everything starts growing again. Now, you need to understand that sometimes you may be ready, but it's wintertime for your wife!

KEYS for MARRIAGE

Have you ever thought about why a man spends hours involved in a sport? He must be fulfilling some need through it. Instead of fighting against what he finds fulfillment in, you should find out why he's interested in it and, if possible, become a part of it.

*W*ives, bless your husbands by getting involved in their recreational activities. If he likes to play tennis, then learn how to play tennis. If he likes to jog, then jog with him sometimes. If he likes football, learn how to throw and catch the ball. Play his game and you'll win your game.

When a woman asks you to hold her,
she doesn't want to go to bed, she wants
affection. Now, if you hold her long enough,
you just may get rewarded!

A lot of women get sex over with quickly because no affection was involved. They feel as if their husbands have used them like a piece of meat. I say to you men: May that never be so among us.

*M*en, pay attention:
Affection and sex are not the same.
If you're not sure how to be affectionate,
ask your wife. You'll be amazed
by her responses.

So husbands ought to love their own wives as their own bodies; he who loves his wife loves himself. For no one ever hated his own flesh, but nourishes and cherishes it, just as the Lord does the church" (Ephesians 5:28–29).

Men, do you know that just pushing the shopping cart patiently in the grocery store is a sign of affection? Helping her cook is being affectionate. Tell her, "Honey, I'll cut up the onions. Let my eyes be the ones that sting."

That's affection!

But I say to you, love your enemies, bless those who curse you, do good to those who hate you, and pray for those who spitefully use you and persecute you" (Matthew 5:44). Sometimes, the only way you can love your spouse, even when he or she seems like the enemy, is by choosing to do so.

$\mathcal{W}$e are to follow Christ's example of
love. While we were yet sinners, He died
for us. He looked beyond our fault
and saw our need.

$\mathscr{T}$rue love is not the kind of love you talk about. It's the kind of love you get to be about.

$\mathcal{L}$ove responds; it does not react. When you react, you blurt out things without thinking. By that time, you've said something hurtful and wounded a spirit, usually the one belonging to the person you love the most. Take a deep breath and count to ten.

Whenever your love is based on a specific reason, then the foundation of your relationship rests upon a condition. Read the fine print: terms and conditions are subject to change.

$\mathscr{Y}$our spouse's face, weight, body, attitude, and emotions are all going to change. Yet, when you love your spouse with agape love—God's kind of love—your love remains the same. Conditions change, but true love is unconditional.

When you assign roles within your marriage, you set up expectations. Expectations cause needless aggravation. Aggravation causes disappointments, which lead to frustration and arguments. Arguments lead to bitterness and strife, which lead to a strained relationship. A strained relationship endangers fellowship....

When the fellowship is endangered,
you jeopardize your marriage.
True love expects nothing in return.

After that, [Jesus] *poured water into a basin and began to wash the disciples' feet, and to wipe them with the towel with which He was girded"* (John 13:5). Seek to serve, not to be served. Jesus didn't ask whose job it was to wash feet. He didn't follow traditional roles; He simply responded to the need.

*D*on't expect one person to do all the cooking, washing, or cleaning. If you don't expect your spouse to do those things, then when he or she doesn't do them, how can you be disappointed? When your spouse chooses to bless you by doing something unexpected, you'll be more inclined to be thankful and appreciative.

A role within a marriage should be a temporary responsibility based on the ability of the one who is able to respond to the need at that given moment. Responsibility is determined by availability and capability.

*I*f you see water on the floor, don't just stand there and think, "Well that's my wife's job. She does the mopping." No, you saw it, so you respond. If you have the ability to respond, then it's your responsibility.

123

To the weak I became as weak, that I might win the weak. I have become all things to all men, that I might by all means save some" (1 Corinthians 9:22). Becoming *"all things"* should be the principle that rules your roles in your marriage.

When things become more important than God and more important than your spouse, the result will always be problems within your home.

We know that sex is a temporary action and is subject to constant change. Since it is always changing, you can't trust it. If you can't put your trust in it, you know you're in trouble when you try to build your relationship upon it.

Sex does not produce commitment. If you don't believe me, ask a prostitute. Sex is a result of commitment in marriage. If your sexual relationship alone doesn't make your marriage, then it can't break it either.

When you say something to your spouse, you have to remember that your spouse may hear his or her interpretation of what you said based upon his or her personal history, and this may be quite different from what you actually meant.

Keys for Marriage

Let your fountain be blessed, and rejoice with the wife of your youth" (Proverbs 5:18). This verse is not saying to enjoy your wife when she is young and then go looking for somebody else. Your wife is supposed to be even better and sweeter to you as you both get older. Grow old gracefully together.

As a loving deer and a graceful doe, let her breasts satisfy you at all times; and always be enraptured with her love" (Proverbs 5:19). Your wife's breasts should satisfy you for how long? *"At all times."* That means that at no time should anyone else's breasts satisfy you.

Men, in order to learn how to love your wives, you first have to find out how Christ loved His church by studying His ultimate manual on love, the Bible.

God does not compare your marriage to that of your brother, sister, parents, or friends. He compares your marriage to Christ and His church. That is the standard.

*H*usbands, the highest witness for Christ that you can give is loving your wife as He loved the church. We need real men in our communities—men of the Word who know what true love is.

$\mathcal{Y}$our wife wants to hear, "I love you. You're beautiful. You're so precious to me." Your husband doesn't need to hear anything; just rub his head and touch his neck when he's driving, and he's in heaven. So, talk to your wife, or give your husband physical affection.

She who is married cares…how she may please her husband" (1 Corinthians 7:34). Wives, you don't need to wait for your husband to initiate sexual relations.

*Y*our wife didn't forfeit her dreams and aspirations when she married you. She has basic needs and desires to feel successful and personally satisfied in her life, just as you do. Find out what her dreams are and be supportive of her goals.

KEYS for MARRIAGE

$\mathcal{Y}$ou must accept the fact that the person you married is not exactly like you. Yet when the differences between your spouse and yourself press together, they will form the precious gem your marriage was always meant to be.

Husbands, love your wives, just as Christ also loved the church and gave Himself for her, that He might...present her to Himself a glorious church, not having spot or wrinkle" (Ephesians 5:25–27).

$\mathcal{M}$en, at the end of each day, go to God and say, "I present my wife to You. How did I do today in removing the 'spots and wrinkles'? What could I do better?" That's your job and priority as a husband, every day of your life.

Your wedding ring represents to the whole world that no matter where you go by yourself, you belong to and are committed to another and are not looking for anybody else. Never leave home without wearing it.

There are things your husband can do that you cannot do, or there are things your wife can do that you cannot do. You should not try to compete with each other, but complete each other. Don't compete—complete.

Husbands, in the same way be considerate as you live with your wives, and treat them with respect as the weaker partner and as heirs with you of the gracious gift of life, so that nothing will hinder your prayers" (1 Peter 3:7 NIV).

There are some things in life no one can afford, and having your prayers hindered is one of them. Be kind, caring, compassionate, sensitive, and attentive to your wife's needs. God is more important than your wife, yet He made having your prayers heard contingent on your relationship with her! Love your wife—protect your prayers.

The male is the foundation of the human family. If the male leaves the home, or if he neglects his responsibility, you have a house built on sand. The rafters rock when the pressures come because the man isn't there.

$\mathcal{M}$any men need to live like the foundation they were created to be. Keep the home steady so your wife and children can always lean on you and know that you aren't going to crack.

$\mathcal{T}$he foundation of a building is important, but it's not more important than the other parts of the structure. The foundation can't perform all the functions itself; for example, only the roof can keep you dry. It's the same way with the human family. The foundation is crucial, but the rest of the family is essential also.

A selfish person wants all the glory, all the credit, all the recognition, all the attention, all the power, all the authority, all the rights, and all the privileges. But a person of love wants others to share what he has.

A virtuous woman is a crown to her husband" (Proverbs 12:4 KJV). The crown of a king is his glory. Many people think that a good wife is just the queen to her king (her husband), but he is only a king because she is the crown of his glory.

Your lips, O my spouse, drip as the honeycomb; honey and milk are under your tongue; and the fragrance of your garments is like the fragrance of Lebanon" (Song of Solomon 4:11). Your wife hungers for the sweetness of your words. Speak your thoughts—she needs it.

$\mathcal{I}$t is through worship and communion with God that a man receives his life's vision, vocation, and work. Some men have forgotten that worship takes precedence over work. When your work interferes with your worship, you cease to fulfill the purpose of a real man.

*A*ny man who would want to inhibit the progress of his spouse just to prove his superiority has an inferiority complex. A man who knows who he is doesn't need to prove himself. He understands that his wife has her own self-esteem, so he encourages her to develop her potential to the fullest.

*W*ives, do you know how many men are where they are today because their helpmates made sure they got there? Whatever a man is not, his wife can help him become.

The secret to staying in love is to keep finding things within your spouse to fall in love with over and over again.

Always be enraptured with her love" (Proverbs 5:19). The responsibility for staying enraptured is not up to your spouse, although he or she has a big part to play. The responsibility is your own.

Let this mind be in you which was also in Christ Jesus" (Philippians 2:5). If the husband and wife both have the same attitude as Christ Jesus, then their relationship is based on selfless giving, sacrifice, service, and forgiveness.

When a husband and wife understand and value each other's purposes, they can have a rewarding relationship, and they can blend their unique designs harmoniously for God's glory.

The Bible equips us to be the husbands and wives we were designed to be. Be a person of the Word as you continue to seek and fulfill God's purposes for your marriage.

About the Author

*D*r. Myles Munroe is an international motivational speaker, best-selling author, educator, leadership mentor, and consultant for government and business. Traveling extensively throughout the world, Dr. Munroe addresses critical issues affecting the full range of human, social, and spiritual development. The central theme of his message is the transformation of followers into leaders and the maximization of individual potential.

Founder and president of Bahamas Faith Ministries International (BFMI), a multidimensional organization headquartered in Nassau, Bahamas, Dr. Munroe is also the founder and executive producer of a number of radio and television programs aired worldwide. He has a B.A. from Oral Roberts University, an M.A. from the University of Tulsa, and has been awarded a number of honorary doctoral degrees.

Dr. Munroe and his wife, Ruth, travel as a team and are involved in teaching seminars together. Both are leaders who minister with sensitive hearts and international vision. They are the proud parents of two college graduates, Charisa and Chairo (Myles, Jr.).

THE ISLANDS OF THE
bahamas

For Information on Religious Tourism
e-mail: ljohnson@bahamas.com
1.800.224.3681

www.worship.bahamas.com

These inspirational quotes from best-selling author Dr. Myles Munroe
on leadership, single living, marriage, and prayer can be applied
to your life in powerful and practical ways.

Keys for Leadership: ISBN: 978-1-60374-029-6 • Gift • 160 pages
Keys for Living Single: ISBN: 978-1-60374-032-6 • Gift • 160 pages
Keys for Marriage: ISBN: 978-1-60374-030-2 • Gift • 160 pages
Keys for Prayer: ISBN: 978-1-60374-031-9 • Gift • 160 pages

WHITAKER
HOUSE

www.whitakerhouse.com